No Room for the Nativity

Vicki Howie and Estelle Corke

Barney waved 'goodbye' to the animals at Hilltop Farm.

'Hurry up, Dad!' he called. 'Miss Bright says we're going to act our nativity play today ...'

'... It's all about baby Jesus being born in a stable.'

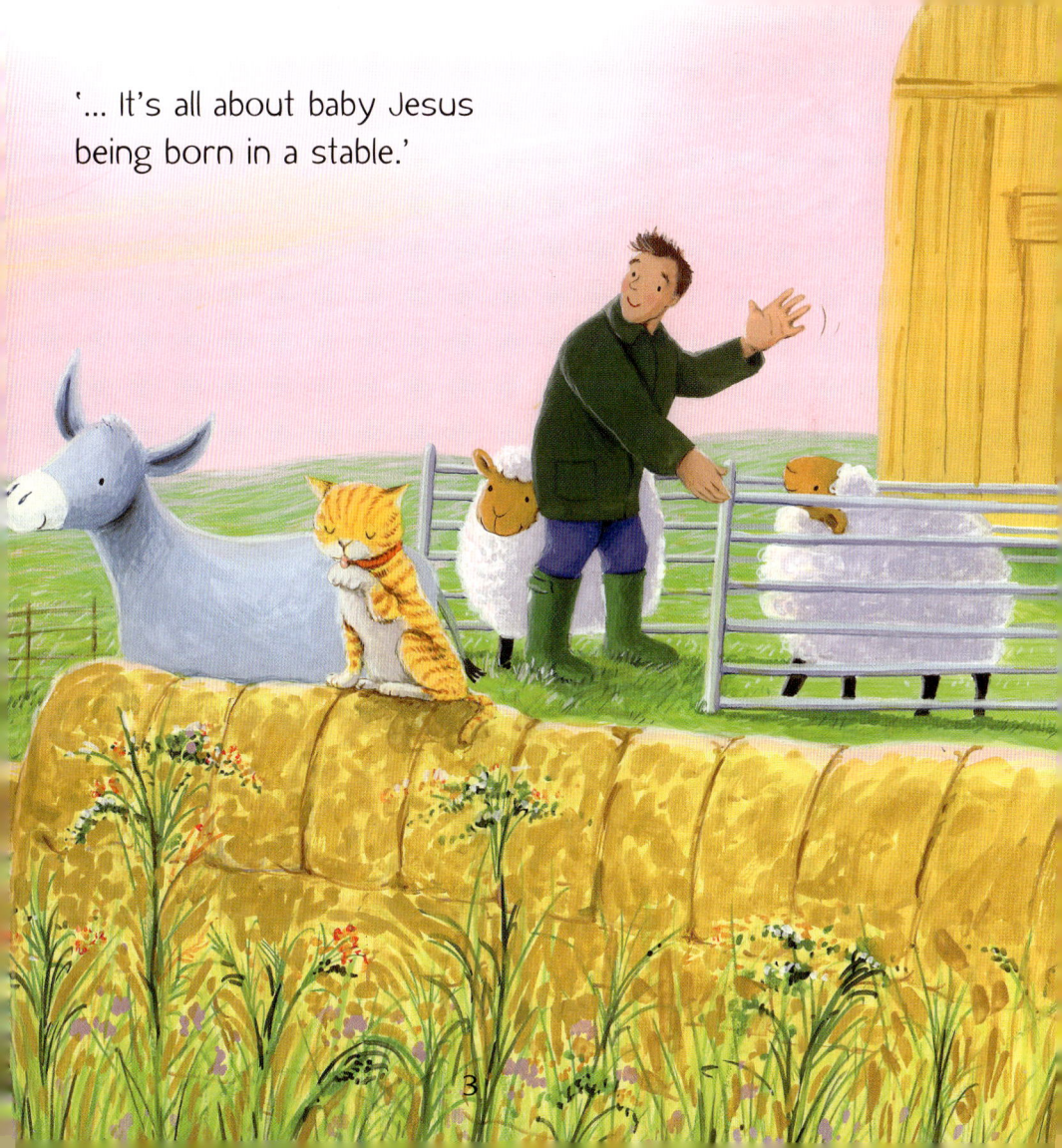

At playgroup, the children were choosing costumes from the dressing-up basket.

'I've got a pair of angel wings!' cried Abigail.

'Look at me! I'm going to be Joseph!' said Freddie, walking with a big stick.

'And I'm going to be Mary in this blue head scarf,' said Jenny.

'Look at us!' cried the twins. 'We can be the donkey!'
Barney looked in the basket, but he couldn't find any more animal costumes.

'Never mind, Barney,' said Miss Bright. 'Perhaps you could be the innkeeper? That's a very important part …'

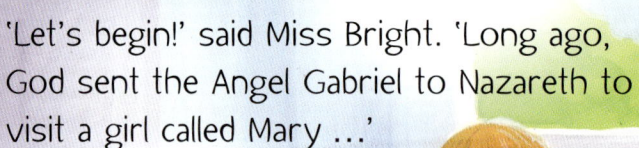

'Let's begin!' said Miss Bright. 'Long ago, God sent the Angel Gabriel to Nazareth to visit a girl called Mary …'

Jenny pretended to be Mary sweeping her floor.

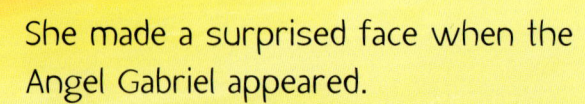

She made a surprised face when the Angel Gabriel appeared.

'Don't be afraid, it's good news!' announced Abigail in her angel voice.

'You are going to have a baby! He will be the Son of God, and you must call Him Jesus.'

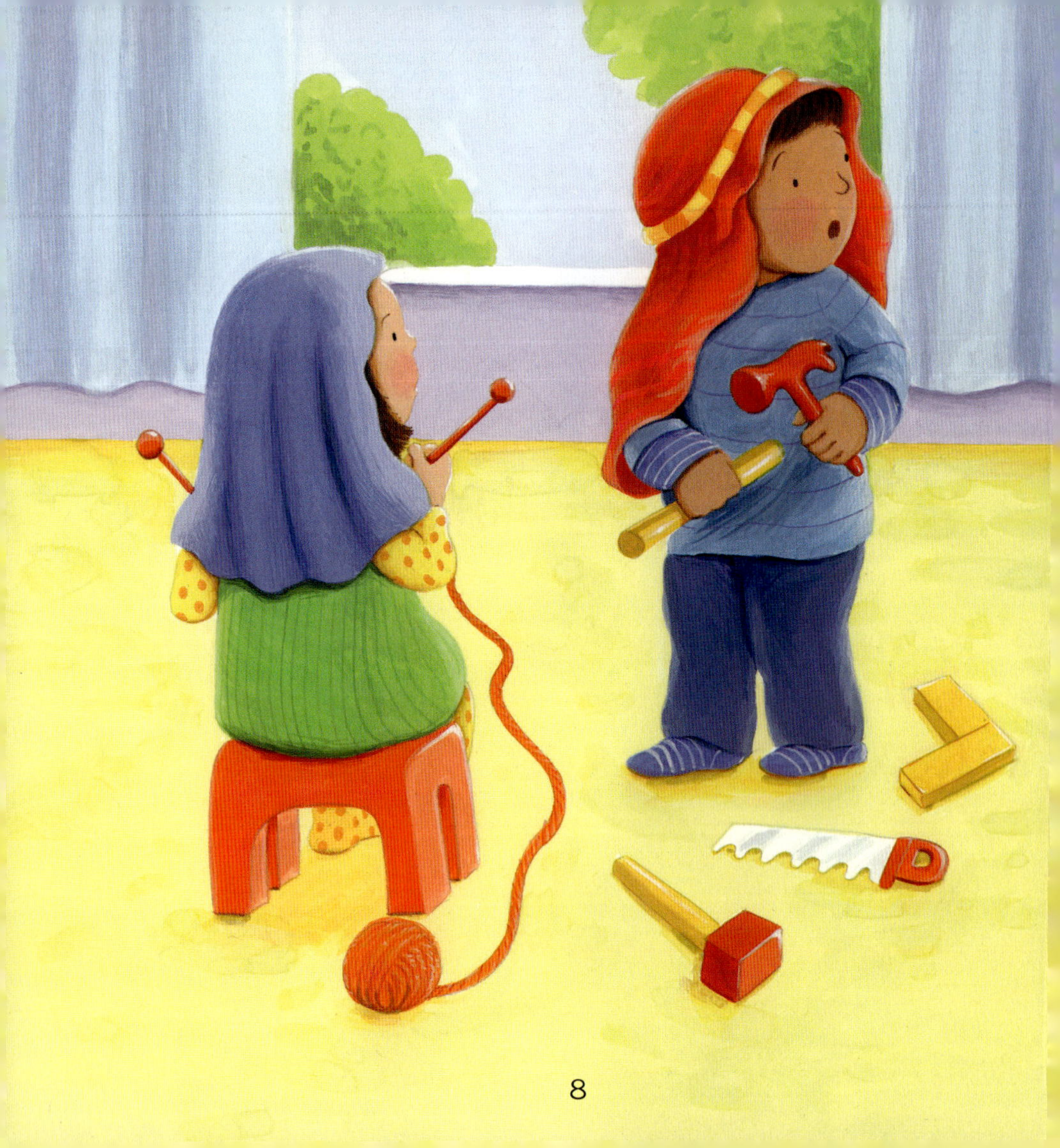

Mary and Joseph pretended to get ready for baby Jesus.

Then George marched across like a soldier.

'You must travel all the way to Bethlehem to be counted,' he ordered. 'The Emperor says so.'

'Oh, no! It's a long way to Bethlehem,' said Mary.

Jenny and Freddie walked around slowly while everyone sang about the little donkey that carried Mary to Bethlehem. Barney wished that they could have a real donkey in their play.

'Knock, knock!' said Joseph. 'Have you a room for the night?'

'No room, no room!' chorused all the children.

'Knock, knock!' said Joseph again. 'Mary is very tired. She is going to have her baby soon.'

'No room, no room!'

Before long there was a real knock on the door. It was going home time already!

'Can we show our play to the Mums and Dads?' asked Barney.

'I wish we could,' said Miss Bright, 'but there isn't room to squeeze everyone in. I'm so sorry, Barney.'

13

'There must be somewhere we could do our play,' Barney said to Dad.

They asked at the community hall ... and then they knocked on one door ... and another ...

But everywhere they went, people shook their heads and said, 'I'm sorry ...'

'... We're very busy ... right up until Christmas.'

'Oh, no!' said Barney. 'It's just like the story. There's no room for the nativity!'

Back at the farm, Barney helped Dad to feed the sheep.
 'Wait! I've had an idea!' said Barney. 'We could do our play in this barn. Could we, Dad?'
 'Ah, I'm not too sure …' Dad hesitated.
 'But Miss Bright says Christmas is all about being kind to others! Oh, please say "yes", Dad!'

'Well, I suppose …
Yes, of course you
can!' said Dad, smiling.
'As long as no one
minds the animals!'

On the day of the play, Dad put the animals safely in their pens and Miss Bright helped the children to dress up. Jenny brought her doll to be baby Jesus.

She wrapped it up in a shawl and hid it near the manger.

'Is everyone ready for our dress rehearsal?' asked Miss Bright.

'Where are the twins?' asked Barney.

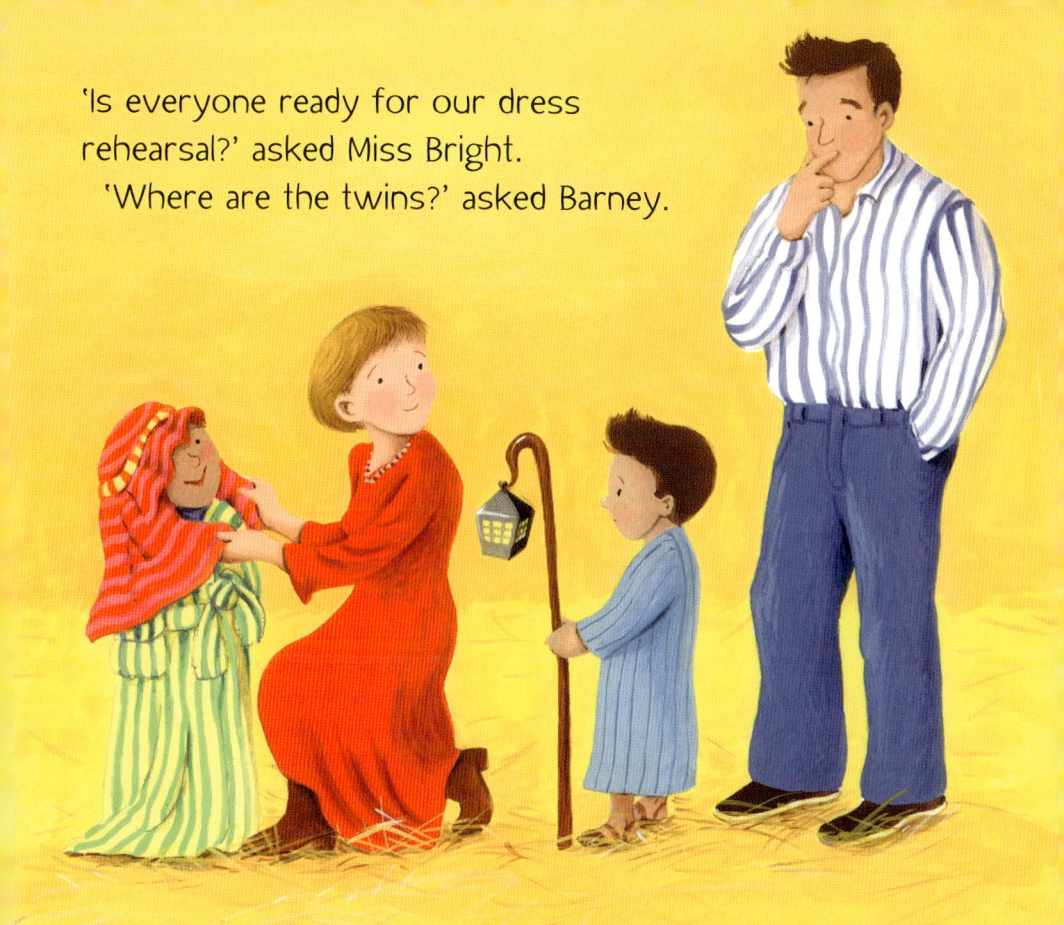

'I'm sorry to say they're poorly,' explained Miss Bright, 'so we'll just have to manage without our donkey.'

'What a shame!' said Dad. 'But I might be able to help ...'

After the rehearsal, the children lined up outside in the yard. Barney peeked through the barn door. He could just see the backs of all the Mums and Dads, brothers and sisters and Grannies and Grandpas who were waiting to see their play.

'God bless you, everyone!' whispered Miss Bright. 'Speak up, and don't forget to smile!'

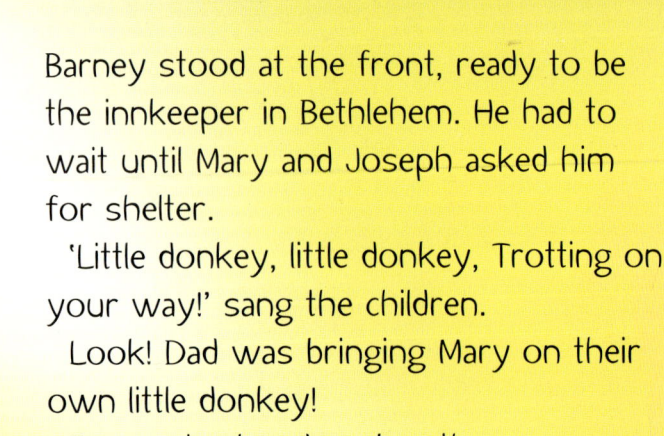

Barney stood at the front, ready to be the innkeeper in Bethlehem. He had to wait until Mary and Joseph asked him for shelter.

'Little donkey, little donkey, Trotting on your way!' sang the children.

Look! Dad was bringing Mary on their own little donkey!

Barney took a deep breath.

'You can stay the night in my barn,' he said, 'because there's no room at the inn.'

Everybody cheered and clapped because it really was Barney's barn!

23

Now it was time for baby
Jesus to be born.

A hush fell as Jenny cuddled her doll, and then placed him very gently in the manger.

'It's a little boy,' said Freddie in his Joseph voice.

'We will call him Jesus,' said Jenny in her Mary voice.

'Glory to God in the highest!' sang all the angels.

Abigail's wings sparkled in the light as she told the shepherds to go and worship the baby.

26

At the end, Miss Bright thanked Dad and Barney for being so kind.

'You opened the barn doors and made room for the nativity,' she said.

'Just like the innkeeper ... and that's me!' added Barney, and everyone clapped and clapped.

Copyright © 2016 Anno Domini Publishing
www.ad-publishing.com
Text copyright © 2016 Vicki Howie
Illustrations copyright © 2016 Estelle Corke

Publishing Director: Annette Reynolds
Art Director: Gerald Rogers
Pre-production Manager: Doug Hewitt

All rights reserved

Printed and bound in China

Published 2016 by CWR
Waverley Abbey House, Waverley Lane, Farnham, Surrey, GU9 8EP, UK
Registered Charity No. 294387
Registered Limited Company No. 1990308
For a list of National Distributors, visit www.cwr.org.uk/distributors